VIOLA

CHRISTMAS FAVORITES

Solos and String Orchestra Arrangements
Correlated with Essential Elements String Method

Arranged by
LLOYD CONLEY

Welcome to Essential Elements Christmas Favorites! There are two versions of each selection in this versatile book. The SOLO version appears in the beginning of your book. The STRING ORCHESTRA arrangements of each song follows. The supplemental recording (CD or Cassette) or string orchestra PIANO PART may be used as an accompaniment for solo performance. Use these recordings when playing solos for friends and family.

Solo Pg.	String Arr. Pg.	Title	Correlated with Essential Elements
3	14	Jingle Bells	Book 1, page 20
4	15	Up On The Housetop	Book 1, page 27
5	16	The Hanukkah Song	Book 1, page 27
6	17	We Wish You A Merry Christmas	Book 1, page 34
7	18	A Holly Jolly Christmas	Book 1, page 41
8	19	Frosty The Snow Man	Book 1, page 41
9	20	Rockin' Around The Christmas Tree	Book 1, page 42
10	21	Jingle-Bell Rock	Book 2, page 19
11	22	Silver Bells	Book 2, page 19
12	23	Let It Snow! Let It Snow! Let It Snow!	Book 2, page 32
13	24	White Christmas	Book 2, page 34

ISBN 978-0-7935-8392-8

HAL•LEONARD®
CORPORATION

7777 W. BLUEMOUND RD. P.O. BOX 13819 MILWAUKEE, WI 53213

00868012

JINGLE BELLS

VIOLA
Solo

Words and Music by J. PIERPONT
Arranged by LLOYD CONLEY

Copyright © 1997 by HAL LEONARD CORPORATION
International Copyright Secured   All Rights Reserved

UP ON THE HOUSETOP

VIOLA
Solo

Words and Music by B.R. HANDY
Arranged by LLOYD CONLEY

Up on the house - top —— rein - deer pause, Out jumps

good old San - ta Claus; Down through the

chim - ney with lots of toys, All for the lit - tle ones,

Christ - mas joys. Ho, ho, ho! Who would - n't

go! Ho, ho, ho! Who would - n't

go! Up on the house - top, click, click,

click, Down through the chim - ney with good

Saint Nick.

THE HANUKKAH SONG

VIOLA
Solo

Traditional
Arranged by LLOYD CONLEY

WE WISH YOU A MERRY CHRISTMAS

VIOLA
Solo

Traditional English Folksong
Arranged by LLOYD CONLEY

A HOLLY JOLLY CHRISTMAS

VIOLA
Solo

Music and Lyrics by JOHNNY MARKS
Arranged by LLOYD CONLEY

00868012

FROSTY THE SNOW MAN

VIOLA
Solo

Words and Music by
STEVE NELSON and JACK ROLLINS
Arranged by LLOYD CONLEY

ROCKIN' AROUND THE CHRISTMAS TREE

VIOLA
Solo

Music and Lyrics by JOHNNY MARKS
Arranged by LLOYD CONLEY

00868012

JINGLE-BELL ROCK

VIOLA
Solo

Words and Music by
JOE BEAL and JIM BOOTHE
Arranged by LLOYD CONLEY

00868012

SILVER BELLS
From the Paramount Picture THE LEMON DROP KID

VIOLA
Solo

Words and Music by
JAY LIVINGSTON and RAY EVANS
Arranged by LLOYD CONLEY

LET IT SNOW! LET IT SNOW! LET IT SNOW!

VIOLA
Solo

Words by SAMMY CAHN
Music by JULE STYNE
Arranged by LLOYD CONLEY

Oh the weath-er out-side is fright-ful But the fire is so de-light-ful, And since we've no place to go, Let it snow! Let it snow! Let it snow! It does-n't show signs of stop-ing, And I brought some corn for pop-ping, The lights are turned way down low, Let it snow! Let it snow! Let it snow! When we fi-nal-ly kiss good-night, How I'll hate go-ing out in the storm! But if you'll real-ly hold me tight All the way home I'll be warm. The fire is slow-ly dy-ing And my dear we're still good-bye-ing, But as long as you love me so, Let it snow! Let it snow! Let it snow! When we snow!

00868012

WHITE CHRISTMAS
From the Motion Picture Irving Berlin's HOLIDAY INN

VIOLA
Solo

Words and Music by IRVING BERLIN
Arranged by LLOYD CONLEY

00868012

JINGLE BELLS

VIOLA
String Orchestra Arrangement

Words and Music by J. PIERPONT
Arranged by LLOYD CONLEY

00868012

UP ON THE HOUSETOP

VIOLA
String Orchestra Arrangement

Words and Music by B.R. HANDY
Arranged by LLOYD CONLEY

00868012

THE HANUKKAH SONG

VIOLA
String Orchestra Arrangement

Traditional
Arranged by LLOYD CONLEY

00868012

WE WISH YOU A MERRY CHRISTMAS

VIOLA
String Orchestra Arrangement

Traditional English Folksong
Arranged by LLOYD CONLEY

A HOLLY JOLLY CHRISTMAS

VIOLA
String Orchestra Arrangement

Music and Lyrics by JOHNNY MARKS
Arranged by LLOYD CONLEY

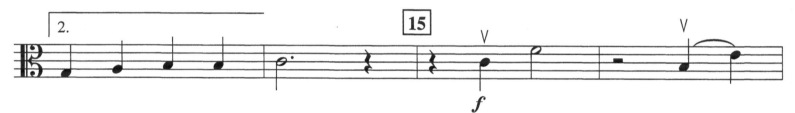

Frosty the Snow Man

Words and Music by
STEVE NELSON and **JACK ROLLINS**
Arranged by LLOYD CONLEY

VIOLA
String Orchestra Arrangement

ROCKIN' AROUND THE CHRISTMAS TREE

VIOLA
String Orchestra Arrangement

Music and Lyrics by JOHNNY MARKS
Arranged by LLOYD CONLEY

JINGLE-BELL ROCK

VIOLA
String Orchestra Arrangement

Words and Music by
JOE BEAL and JIM BOOTHE
Arranged by LLOYD CONLEY

Medium Rock

00868012

SILVER BELLS
From the Paramount Picture THE LEMON DROP KID

VIOLA
String Orchestra Arrangement

Words and Music by
JAY LIVINGSTON and **RAY EVANS**
Arranged by LLOYD CONLEY

LET IT SNOW! LET IT SNOW! LET IT SNOW!

VIOLA
String Orchestra Arrangement

Words by SAMMY CAHN
Music by JULE STYNE
Arranged by LLOYD CONLEY

WHITE CHRISTMAS
From the Motion Picture Irving Berlin's HOLIDAY INN

**Words and Music by
IRVING BERLIN**
Arranged by LLOYD CONLEY

VIOLA
String Orchestra Arrangement